G

GW00643463

PAUL F. GORMAN

Author of
Awareness Itself
Releasing the Universe Within
The Great Need
I Am (A Meditation)
I Am Now (A Meditation)
One
The Miracle Self
The Giving Self
Healing of The Body
The Way of Awakening
Satisfied with God Alone
Bringing Forth the Presence of God
Anyone Can Demonstrate Infinity
The Impersonal Self
The Inner Sanctuary
The Seven Spiritual Steps to Solving Any Problem
Opening the Windows of Heaven
Only God Is
The Fully Manifest Presence
That Which You Seek

VINE PRESS
NAPA, CALIFORNIA

On-Minute God Experiences
Copyright © 2018 by Paul F. Gorman

FIRST EDITION

ISBN-13: 978-0-9990218-9-7
ISBN-10: 0-9990218-9-3

Published by Vine Press
Napa, California

www.miracleself.com

Available from Amazon.com and other book stores worldwide

Rise in consciousness – this is the entire secret.

As consciousness rises, detaching from and leaving
belief behind, ever greater degrees of heaven
are visible through the unconditioned mind.

"As in heaven so on earth."

The earth and all its people, creatures and conditions
are witnessed unconditioned, whole and harmonious,
love and union of all emerging through the fog
of false sense.

Indeed, "As in heaven so on earth" emerges as the one
reality – the bondage of false material sense dispelled,
the unconditioned experience of Man, Earth and
Universe harmonious, peaceful and free, in love.

Paul F. Gorman

One-Minute
God Experiences

All is God.

We could all sit under a tree somewhere beautiful, ponder this one statement—All is God—feel its truth, let it live and become tangible in us, and sooner or later, heaven would be evident as earth.

All is God. I wonder how many hear that over and over, and still believe it to be a benefit to the personal self. Such belief does nothing except shut God out of experience.

God is not "within" existence—within you, within mind, within flesh, within form, within condition. If within-ness were true, without-ness would also have to be true. The realization of omnipresence wipes out belief in an inner vs.

an outer.

God is *presence,* not *power* as we understand power to be. *Power,* as the hypnotized state understands it, is a power *over* something. It is cause and effect.

In a belief state of awareness, I can say I have the power of decision, the power of choice, that I have power over people, things and conditions less powerful than I.

But in that case I am living with belief in multiple powers and I am left exposed to many greater powers that are able to dominate me—to cause me injury or disease, lack, limitation, poverty, failure, unhappiness, exposure to danger, old age, and eventually death.

None of this is of truth. God is one; therefore only one power exists—the power of *presence,* of *is.*

> *God* is, *existence* is. *All that is made* is God itself. *And because the inner is the outer and*

the outer is the inner, every "part" of all that exists is the full presence of God—the omnipresence, infinity, omniscience and omni-activity of perfect, indivisible, inseparable God presence.

"All things were made by him; and without him was not anything made that was made." (John 1:3) Understand this statement as being current, as being of *is,* of *now.* All things *are* made by him and, in fact, *are* God itself, and without him, without God, is not anything made or is not anything existent that is existent. And, "He was in the world, and the world was made by him [the world is God] and the world knew him not." (John 1:10)

Human sense, human consciousness or awareness, material consciousness or awareness cannot see the God that is right in front of it, all around it, that *is* it. Why? Because as human or material awareness, we are closed to that which *is.* We are attached to the appearance, to that which we believe to be real, and while we are attached to that which seems to be, we are not free, and God is not free in us so that we can experience God as it is. So, remember, any attachment whatsoever, any belief whatsoever is blocking God from our experience, is making it impossible for us to see that which is. We are closed up. Our eyes are blind.

But as we detach, as we live free in spirit, free in God awareness, in God presence, then God is free in us to reveal itself as the true image and likeness. God must be free in us.

The moment we are closed up in any way, attached in any way, believe anything to any degree, God isn't free in us. God is imprisoned in us, and it feels to us as if God is nowhere to be found, that God has deserted us. Well, no, we have deserted God by having false idols, by being involved in that which seems to be, instead of that which *is*. We're about our own business. We are about the human, personal-self, world business instead of about the Father's business. Only by being about the Father's business are we open and receptive to the revelation, the visibility of all that God *is* as all that we experience.

Realize that whatever we experience, there God is—through sense—as that very thing, that very person, condition, amount, place, business, circumstance, family, home. Do you see? It does not matter what we are aware of. If God is free in us, then what we are aware of is the image and likeness of God as person, thing and condition. Another way of describing this is "the healing consciousness."

God *is*. God is all of all, but if we are aware as human sense, personal self sense, material sense, if we're attached, nothing we can do—including all the truth study we could ever do, all the meditation and all the silence we could ever sit in—is able to reveal that which *is* because we are not *being* that which is.

We have to *be that which is* in order to see it, experience it, have it. We have to *be infinity* in order to see and to have infinity of all form, all awareness, all amount, all person.

Get a deeper sense of the fact that God is all of all. We need to wipe out any belief that we have heard this before. We haven't heard a single truth until we are demonstrating it—until we see it, until we have it; until it is all around us, until it fills our life.

Let us never allow belief to convince us that we have heard this, that we would rather have something "new." The whole world is new every moment. You are new every moment. Your awareness is new every moment. You are the fresh manna every moment. However, if you are not witnessing this newness, the way of witnessing it is this:

Realize that God is all of all. There is no "part" of you—no matter how you describe yourself or your mind or your body or your universe (and everything in it) to be—that is not the entirety of God.

God is not within; God is all of all. Realize this of your body. God is this very body (all of it), not *within* this body. That is true as well, but within-ness does not mean physically within; it means the essence, the purity, the absolute all of all of whatever is being sensed, in this case the body. The body you have and you see, hear, taste, touch, and smell, this seemingly very physical body, isn't physical. It is God; it is spiritual, incorporeal.

You are incorporeal; all is incorporeal. The entire sensed universe is incorporeality sensing itself. We sense objectively, but this does not mean that we sense *objects*. We have a objective *sense* of that which is one hundred percent incorporeal. *Being* (life and life-form) is incorporeal. Only like sees like, only like *experiences* like. If anything in infinity were corporeal it would be eternally invisible and experience-less to us.

In other words, the fact that we are incorporeal and that we see a universe of life and form proves that all is incorporeal. Do you catch this?

If we were separate and different from God, we would be unable to see the things of God; and because all things are made by him, we would be entirely blind.

This is why, when we *believe* that we are separate and different from God, we cannot see the image and likeness of God.

You are incorporeal. The body is incorporeal. We have a deep belief about it being corporeal, being physical, and so that is our experience. Nevertheless, all is incorporeal. Incorporeality does not exist within, is not ethereal; it is all of all. Experience, no matter what we belive about it, is incorporeal. For instance, when you touch your arm, you have a seemingly physical experience, but it is one hundred percent incorporeal—the palpable incorporeal; incorporeal visibility, tangibility; actual form, function, experience.

This presence of you, and of your hand and arm is the all-of-all of God. From the deepest atomic level of awareness, to the cellular and all the way "out" to the skin; and then (because you have no edge to you, even though sense tries to convince you that you do) out into your universe, all is the omnipresence, the oneness of God that you are.

You are consciousness itself, omnipresence itself. This being true, tell me, where is an edge to consciousness itself, omnipresence itself? Where is an inner versus an outer? Where is different substance, form and function? Where is the atomic versus the cellular? Where is the cellular versus the muscular, the bones, the blood, the skin? Where is the edge of your body and then out into the body of your room? Where is that separation in God, in consciousness itself, in omnipresence? None of these edges, opposites and differences exist. You are, your mind is, your body is, your entire universe and all it constitutes are consciousness itself, omnipresence, incorporeality.

Rest now in incorporeality. Withdraw your senses, your attention, your interest from the body, from things, from anything you can name, define, any objective experience, to incorporeality or omnipresence. Spend three or four minutes doing this.

(A few minutes contemplation and release)

Becoming a state of emptiness and receptivity for the God experience depends on our release from that which seems to be, into omnipresence, consciousness itself. Spend three or four minutes really letting go of everything of your sensed self and sinking into the peace and the quiet, the infinity of incorporeality, omnipresence, spirit.

(Five minutes silence)

The Omni-Activity of God

Realize the omni-activity of God. It is the Father's good pleasure to give you the kingdom just as it is the sun's good pleasure to give the sunbeam the kingdom. The sun is proactive, omni-active. None of the sunbeam's sunshine depends on her. The fullness of her experience is her emptiness and receptivity, her impersonal self, yielded entirely to the sun itself. In this state of existence, she witnesses all that the sun is and has as all that her world is and has.

In this very way, let us realize that our presence, the presence of our all of all, is the presence, the power, of God—the omni-activity of God.

Nothing Is Solid

Nothing is solid. Look at an object in your room. Sense testimony infused with belief suggests that the object is solid. As you observe it, it is as it always has been in your appearance world. You can turn your gaze away from it, look at something else, then turn back to the object, and it is still there, looking exactly the same to you.

But nothing is *still there*. No person, thing or condition is solid, local, objectified, is *still there* when you look back at him, her or it. Not even the world or universe is *still there*. God is omnipresence, not an object, and omnipresence is not solid, structural or fixed, and cannot be.

Nothing of the experience of omnipresence, even objectively sensed (as all is at our current level of awareness) is solid, structural, fixed.

You are not fixed. Your body is not fixed. Your family, home, business, money, city and world are not fixed. All is omnipresence—all that God is and has; and all is omni-activity, the ever-new presence of God experienced.

Your body is forever new. Your universe is forever new—brand new, "straight out of God," a brand new God experience every nanosecond (or yoctosecond—one septillionth of a second— the current shortest time measurement).

Of course, the instantaneity of God is immeasurable. Every immeasurable instant is brand new God experience, objectively sensed as the very people, things, conditions, amounts, activities, and places we experience. All is God. God is all of all, and every immeasurable instant all is brand new (just like every instant of sunshine, gravity and electricity is brand new).

The only aspects of experience that give the impression that everything in our lives is *still there,* and, in fact, appearing to get old, tired, withered, decrepit and eventually dead and thrown into the fire, are belief and memory. Memory is a deep aspect of belief but has no foundation, no law, no principle in truth. Put belief and memory aside and realize:

I am omnipresence itself. I am infinity itself. I am eternity itself.

Nothing is fixed. Nothing is the same as it was yesterday or the same as it was one immeasurable instant ago.

Only God is, which is is—*the one constant, the same "yesterday, today and forever".*

God is ever new in experience.

The one constant is ever newly-sensed and realized, the ever-fresh experience of all that God is and has, like the ever-new experience of gravity, electricity and sunshine.

The sunbeam is never *as it was* yesterday, not even as it was one instant ago. The sunbeam is the omni-activity, the omnipresence of the sun which is, in experience, forever pouring out, ever new. No part of the sunbeam can say it is the same as it was yesterday. No part of the sunbeam's mind, body, home, supply, world or universe is the same as it was even one instant ago.

It is exactly the same with us. No part of us, nothing at all of our experience is the same as it was even one immeasurable instant ago. All is new, and that newness, that fresh manna is the *whole* of God being every aspect of our moment-by-moment experience.

This is why the more this truth is realized, the more simple healing becomes. Healing has nothing to do with "us"; healing is the presence of God evidenced. It is the omni-activity of God in our experience, opened to and sensed within. It is evidenced "for us" not by us. God is ever new every immeasurable instant, and that newness does not bring with it the belief of disease, injury, limitation, struggle, fear, age, or death.

Even when we observe what is supposed to be a dead body, that body is full of life. Despite good, bad or even dead appearance, every immeasurable instant is newly full of and is the form of life. That is why even apparently dead bodies can get up and start walking on earth again *when we are in the consciousness of omnipresent, omniactive life (God)*. If we are in the consciousness of appearance, nothing in heaven and earth combined can make a dead body walk again. If we are in human, personal self consciousness, our (or another's) diseased body remains diseased.

A struggling business—or any enterprise—is ever new. It is, from before inception, the finished kingdom of itself and is witnessed as being so in God consciousness. It may take us a few hours to witness it if we are not already in a high enough state of awareness and need to lift, but that is okay; a few hours is good enough. We will infallibly witness it as long as we are detached and disinterested in the appearance, and fully in and interested in God itself—in God as a business? No. As the finished kingdom of customers, clients, transactions, products, services and money? No. As *God,* the finished kingdom of *God.*

In and from this awareness, watch the miracle of the fresh instant becoming more and more evident, objectively sensed. Nothing can resist the presence of God realization—nothing—because nothing else exists but God.

"We" are the resistance to the God experience if we are attached to appearance, if we carry on believing in an experience separate and apart from God, if we are trying to get God to change a business, heal a body, bring love to a family, bring peace to stormy seas and to destructive weather. That is no way of God.

God is God itself alone, so it is when we are being of God itself alone, when we are imbued with God and God imbued with us, when we have no other attachment, no other interest, no other desire, that we are full of God as God is for God, not for anything else. This is when we witness the image and likeness of God. This is when we see miraculous changes, miraculous multiplication of good—of food, dollars, business, love, health, peace. We see and have the true good by the degree of our fullness of God.

The Omni-Activity of God

Let us meditate again, realizing the omni-activity of God *as God is*. Stay released and detached from everything of appearance. Always come naked into God. The minute we bring even a bag of candy with us we are unable to enter the kingdom of God, and God is unable to be free in us to be evident as itself as our experience.

So let us come naked into God and then rest, gently realizing the omni-activity of God as God is as all of all. Deeply rest and relax in the omnipresence and omni-activity that is the truth of your very presence, your very mind, body, and universe. Abandon yourself to God. Truly let go of everything you believe to be you and yours, and let God be free in you.

(Five minutes meditation and silence)

Now, empty of self and yielded to God in this way—empty of personal sense, detached from all that seems to be, receptive to God, receptive to the presence and the omni-activity of God (which is new life, presence, mind, body, and universe and all that these constitute every immeasurable instant)—you are *having* the God experience. You are experiencing and often feeling the activity of the presence of God itself as you.

Because God is omnipresence, the experience we may deem to be within "us," within a physical sense, is not that at all. It is omnipresence. We cannot separate and divide God. We cannot have God in here without having God as the entirety of our universe. It does not matter how we may feel the presence of God, and it does not matter if we do not feel God. As long as we are open and receptive in this way *we are having the God experience.* God *is.* Nothing we do or do not feel makes a difference to what *is.*

As long as we have put aside the personal self and are full of God awareness and are open, receptive, just being still in God, then whether we feel anything or not, we are *consciously having* the God experience. God is released in us and throughout our universe because we have made ourselves consciously available to and for God. God is tangibly omnipresent in and throughout us.

In this experience, the whole of our consciousness—the whole of our universe—is this instant new, fresh, full of God. As long as we remain in God consciousness as we go out into our worlds instead of getting up and immediately looking for objective results, then the image and likeness of the omnipresence and omni-activity of God is infallible.

We will always sense objectively, but we have to stay detached, stay in God, stay as *I* as *I am*. But if we re-attach, we have shut God out in the instant of attachment. Stay detached in God.

I have been working with a number of individuals who are struggling to accept their healings. One in particular, who has been struggling for about six months now, is finding it very difficult to let go of the personal sense of self and of disease and severe pain, and she is desperate to be free of it. She has admitted that honestly she most desires to regain her healthy, pain-free personal self. She wants her personal life fixed so that she can continue living it. She is fully aware of this, but has so far been unable to release her personal sense of self. Each time she calls for help, the pain dissolves within a few minutes at most—not completely, but by eighty to ninety percent.

With others still hanging onto personal sense release is quicker, sometimes instant. However, these individuals continue to struggle in one way or another with evidencing their health. They receive their release as they call for help but are back again within a day or two as they return to a personal sense of life.

The struggle (any unyielding problem) always comes down to one thing—a personal sense of self with a personal problem. The moment we can truly release the personal sense, God is experienced very quickly (if not instantly) and reveals itself as the image and likeness of health, sufficiency and harmony.

I have been experimenting with a simple practice that these individuals who call for help can continue throughout the day. It is working very beautifully, so I want to share it with you here.

One-Minute God Experiences

Here is the practice.

First, lift your awareness into God so that you are prepared and ready for the God experience. You must come naked to God. The healing of disease, lack, limitation, or disharmony of any nature depends on our coming to God *already consciously free of the problem*. We must be sufficiently consciously free of what appears to be, and open in God—even though pain may still be sensed, even though the appearance of the problem may still be sensed, and probably is. Appearance does not matter as long as we are not attached to it, wanting it of itself to change. When we have experienced sufficient release of the personal sense of the problem and attachment to it by lifting into God consciousness, we are ready.

Now have a one-minute God experience:

Simply sit still, empty, aware of God, seeking God, wanting the God experience *as and for what God itself is*—not for anything that you can name or define, but for the God experience *as and for itself alone.* (This is the secret of healing and of evidencing every fulfillment of mind, body and world.)

We can easily hold this receptivity for one minute. Just rest, relax, look up into God, and for one minute make yourself available for the God experience.

(One minute of silent receptivity)

Now, as long as you were sincerely seeking the God experience as and for itself alone, not for anything that you can name or define, you have *had* it. Whether you felt anything or not is not the issue. It is not important.

When I first realized this, I had been sitting for months in a great deal of disease and pain trying to experience healing. I only believed my silence had been effective if I had felt a comforting and encouraging peace or warmth or release within. When I did, I felt satisfied, but when I didn't, I believed my meditation and silence had been ineffective.

One day I was in silence listening as hard as I could and these words came through emphatically: How selfish you are being to judge whether you have had a God experience by the amount of peace you feel or do not feel! I jumped up from my chair and realized, ah, of course, of course! What does it matter if I feel peace or warmth or a release, or not? That is just an *effect* a personal sense of self is feeling. It in itself has nothing to do with the fact that God is all that exists, and besides God, none else exists.

God *is, regardless.* God is what *I am, regardless.* God is all that I am and all that I experience, *re-*

gardless, no matter how I may define it, name it or feel it. Do you see? Even the worst of experiences are in fact God (not *as* they are experienced, but in truth) because God is all that exists, *but I am having a very poor interpretation of it.* Every problem I can ever experience has nothing to do with what it appears to be but is a problem of poor interpretation or translation of God.

This was a huge revelation for me. From that moment I sat in hours of silence not caring whether I felt a single moment of peace. I realized that despite my *sense* of life, the whole creation is actually what this life and body of "me" is, and it is in perfect self-complete, self-sustained and self-maintained order *as and for itself.* Of course, as soon as I stopped caring about feeling peace, I was mostly filled with an abundance of peace.

Do not desire any particular God feeling. Do not measure whether or not you have had a God experience by a feeling or no feeling. You *are having* the full God experience when, like the sunbeam, you are sufficiently empty of self; when you are sincerely released from both the bad and the good of the world (released from the body, released from the problem for this moment or period of meditation and silence) and seeking God *as God is* and for *what* God is; and when the human of you, along with its needs and desires, is out of the equation.

By sufficiently contemplating God, you become a state of emptiness, stillness and spiritual receptivity where you sit in God naked of self, naked of world, naked of things and conditions. Then, for one minute, you look up into God, seek and be open and available for the experience of God as God is—for God to get on with being God in you and as you without "you" taking up space and getting in the way. Then, in this state, whether you feel anything or not, you *have had* the God experience.

This practice is witnessing beautiful results for those who have been struggling. Last Friday, we experienced the greatest release one of them has had in seven months. It was beautiful to witness.

For this individual, it was a major leap into God, and it continues as she continues the practice. Every individual who has adopted it so far is experiencing wonderful fruits. All I have talked to are experiencing greater tangible release and its fruits as they keep practicing the one-minute God experience.

As you adopt the practice, remember that God is omnipresence. Each one-minute God experience "releases" God as your entire universe and everything it constitutes. God is released universally, not just "in you," the physical, local sense of being. For this one-minute conscious God experience, God is free in and through you to be what *it is*—the one mind, one body, one universe, one all of all.

When we know this and then rest in it and trust it, we *see* it. Often we see it very quickly, as long as we stay in God as best we can and do not step back out and go looking for objective results. That will never work. That shuts us right back out of God again. But, like the sunbeam staying in the consciousness of the sun, thereby being and having all that the sun is and has, as we stay in the awareness of God being all of all, even as we're busy in our worlds, and we stop twenty or thirty times a day for a one-minute God experience, we maintain a tangible openness and receptivity to all the health, abundance, harmony and peace of God made evident.

As you start the day like this and then continue, it is very easy to stay in enough God consciousness to be able to regularly stop, maybe contemplate truth for 30 seconds (60 seconds if need be) then for one minute simply rest, relax, and experience God as God is, never once hoping for or waiting for any particular feeling. Leave the entire experience to God as God is. A feeling of peace or warmth or release is almost a bonus; it is a fulfilling *effect,* but it is not God itself. God *is;* God does not depend on the agency of feeling or effect to be evident. The reality and evidence of God is eternally before any particular feeling we may experience. Feeling or no feeling, God *is.* This is the important realization. Drop the belief about and desire for feelings, abandon yourself to God, and let God get on with being

God. This is the way of clear seeing.

Let us have another minute.

(One minute God experience)

Pepper your days and nights with these one-minute God experiences and watch your life transform.

These are not replacements for longer periods of meditation and silence, of course, but they are a practical way of being able to take the God experience into the world with us, even into busy days, to keep ourselves open and receptive to the tangibility of good.

Any of us can find a place to be quiet with God for one minute; and as we realize that God is ever new, completely fresh, visible, tangible as the omnipresence of our experience, every time we consciously open ourselves to God, our vision becomes clearer. Everything we experience becomes ever more clearly seen as the image and likeness of God, ever-new God, ever more evident, tangible, visible good.

Be careful never to seek the image and likeness in itself. We are speaking of the visibility, the tangibility, the newness of the *God* experience, which is then automatically and infallibly witnessed as its image and likeness. But do not get involved in the image and likeness; leave it entirely to God.

Stay in God itself for the experience of God itself. Pepper your days with this practice and watch the miracles that become evident in every category of your experience.

Visit www.miracleself.com/MSBooksOnline.html
to freely read unabridged Miracle Self books
(no email, password or fee is required)

~

The Miracle Self *Monthly Letter* is available free
upon request.

Go to www.miracleself.com for free subscription

26459302R00020

Printed in Poland
by Amazon Fulfillment
Poland Sp. z o.o., Wrocła